The Formation of My Walls

Mary Hale

I0086661

www.WeAreAPS.com

ISBN: 978-1-945145-45-2

APS Publishing
2653 S. Lawndale
Chicago, IL 60623
847-942-6135
www.WeAreAPS.com

Table of Contents

WHEN THE HEART IS DIVIDED,
IT IS NOT STABLE AND
THERE IS MORE ROOM FOR THE
FORMATION OF WALLS.

Introduction

Naturally speaking, the heart is the central chest organ that moves the rest of the body. Without the heart, the body does not function, and we cannot live. Spiritually, the heart represents the central or innermost part of our lives. It has a lot to do with our physical, emotional, intellectual, and moral activities that help us function every day.

The heart acknowledges what it holds – especially its logic or reasoning, as well as its feelings. The heart experiences happiness, joy, sorrow, anger, peace – a wide range of emotions. It reacts when we are feeling high or low; when we love; when we fear; and/or when we hate.

Spiritually, the heart thinks and stores memories. The heart is meant to reason, understand, discern, and give insight. The heart plans, makes commitments, and decisions. It is also the seat of the conscience. On its own, it is wicked and can contaminate our whole life.

"For out of the abundance of the heart the mouth speaks." Matthew 12:34

Chapter 1:

Understanding the Body, Soul, and Spirit

As human beings, we have souls. The word soul means "life". The soul refers to our mind and ego. It refers to our life within ourselves.

Man has three parts: The body, the soul, and the spirit. We have found a body for the physical world. We have a soul for contacting the mental and emotional world. We have a spirit to help our conscience determine the difference between right and wrong. Another way to look at it is that the body is the suit for being in this world. The soul is the awareness of oneself, one's appearance, or one's actions. The spirit is the awareness of God. Love causes affections toward other people or things. Affections originate from our senses.

This is all part of being human. It is the personality of humans that make us conscious and cautious of ourselves. The soul is our will, our intellect and our emotions.

Understanding how these entities function will help us better understand our heart and the reasons why we feel as we do about the situations that occur in our lives.

Chapter 2:

The Connection between the Heart and the Mind

The mind is where our thoughts and feelings come from and the heart is where a deeper awareness of what we feel originates. When the mind is not clear, and the heart is distorted from memories triggered by past traumas, it can destroy relationships. The heart is the source of love, joy, serenity, honor, respect, courage, and patience. The heart is the seat of the soul.

As human beings, our thoughts formulate in the mind, but when it comes to our emotions, it is the human heart that takes over our mind. This begins the flow of the issues of life because "out of the abundance of the heart the mouth speaks" (Matthew 12:34). The heart controls our feelings and emotions. We make decisions based on what is right and wrong, and it is the heart that decides our feelings.

A broken heart is not always the result of a love affair. We love people differently than we love things; however, losing either can cause pain or disappointment, just in different ways. This breakup, detachment, abandonment, or loss can cause physical pain to the heart or chest area, created by emotional stress. The dictionary defines heartbreak as "crushing grief, anguish, or distress". There are a lot of cause and effects of being broken-hearted. Some of us experienced disappointments in our childhood (loss of possessions, jobs, etc.). Whatever the cause, the pain of a broken heart can become a formation of walls.

Chapter 3:

The Effects of Your Walls

When using the word "wall" as a noun, it is a brick or stone structure. When used as a verb, it means to give privacy or protect.

The positive thing about walls is that they are used to protect; the negative thing is that walls can hold us captive. So, while nothing can enter, nothing can leave either. There is a difference between being safe and being trapped.

When this concept is applied to our lives and the way we live, we have a choice between positive and

negative, as well as when to hold on
and when to let go. When walls have
been built in our lives in a negative
way, they become entrapment. When
life holds us captive, it affects our
mind, our body and our soul, which
can leave us spiritually altered.
When we are trapped in our minds,
our hearts do not heal properly
because we hold on to hurt and
disappointment. When our hearts
hurt, it affects our health, so we
become captive, or prisoner in many
ways.

Our hearts are considered to be the
little brain that communicates with
the mind and the body. The heart
and the brain work together in
producing emotions. We go through a
mental process that leads us in life.
Our will is where decisions are
made. The heart is the center of our
character, as well as our mental and
spiritual lives. It is closely connected
to feelings and affection. Joy
originates from the heart; bitterness

and jealousy also stem from the heart.

When our hearts are hurting or broken, we close doors of opportunity from being with our family, friends, and meaningful relationships that were destined to help us through life. We suffer from depression, anxiety, and many other ailments because the doors of opportunity have been closed. We close doors and pull-down shades because the walls are being put up in our life. The doors of opportunity were there, but the heart said 'no', so life was put on hold because we could not get pass the heart of yesterday to move into the future, our destiny. Our destiny has been altered because of our walls, stones of the past, and other issues that have been spoken that we did not have to accept.

As we get older, the bricks and stones turn cold and lifeless. We never got rid of them; instead, we allowed more bricks and stones to enter as an attempt to conceal what became what I call "an abandoned lonely castle". This is our own private jail cell where our minds hold us prisoner.

Chapter 4:

Held
in
Captivity

Did you know that in this jail cell you can become an abuser? You are sick and don't realize it; in need of help, but unaware. It is not necessarily that you need medication, simply to let go of the hurt and disappointment.

"For out of the heart proceed evil thoughts, murders, adulteries, fornications, thefts, false witness, blasphemies."
Matthew 15:19

The corruption starts in the heart and out of the heart the mouth speaks. It is the heart that is wicked; there are evil thoughts from the mind, the heart, the soul, and the spirit.

Think of it this way:
If we were talking about a computer, the computer would be our mind. The thoughts that we type into the computer are our hearts. If they are not edited, but instead saved, they become the hard copy. Our souls store hurt and disappointment in the mind, which holds space in our spirit. The soul does not edit, so the mouth speaks it.

We allow our lives to be put on hold because of what someone has said or done in the past, and we refuse to release it. When our hearts are broken, this can cause us to be challenging to deal with because our moods and behaviors are affected; we are stuck in the past. Most people

who have unresolved life matters
of the heart become controlling
because they do not want to be
hurt again.

Some realize that people are
entitled to live their lives as they
see fit. We understand that people
are not obligated to like us; they
have the choice to leave us. People
can speak badly about us, and
even hate us – it's their right. But
we accept it and move on. We don't
hold on; we let go and move on.

However, there is wickedness in
our hearts that we are unaware of.
We make the mistake of believing
that we love and care a lot more
than we really do. We think that
there is no jealousy or envy in our
hearts. We consider ourselves
better than this behavior. We are
in denial.

The heart, the conscience of man
in his fickle nature, is deceitful

above all things. It is very tricky. Because of hearts, we become self-deceivers, self-destroyers, and delusional. The heart is wicked, deadly, and desperate. We do not know our own hearts, so how can we try to understand the hearts of others, or depend on their love for us?

Chapter 5:
The Aftermath

It is my will that controls my emotions. I can make the decision to go from being mad to glad to sad. But then, I reason with myself to know the difference and what I prefer to feel.

Love is an emotion and lust is a feeling. I know that love is positively the greatest gift of all, but lust fulfills a need. So, if I want to fulfill a need without giving love in return, my heart will feel a negative craving or sense of covetousness, and brings on a lust for sex, control, or power, which are all negative because of their points of origin.

The question must be asked: If I can't give love, but need love, am I able to risk the pain and betrayal that comes with it because of the lust that accompanies my need? This has to be taken into serious consideration because unfortunately, when you choose to indulge, you pass on the same spirit of rejection to the next person. So, there is a restriction and with that restriction comes a motive. With the risk of being wounded in any relationship whether with a parent, child, pet or romance, these actions pull away from love.

Love is a work of courage and forgiveness, give and take. If we build walls of fear, insecurities, weaknesses, unforgiveness, anger, doubt, unbelief, rage and suspicion toward our family, people by using negative words and actions, we will never know the depths and widths of those walls. The devastation of it leaves us numbed by our actions and the actions of others. This can cause mental and physical harm and negatively effect our lives at some point or another regarding our state of mind. It can change our entire outlook on life.

When we are emotionally scarred, our mind and heart suffer, which effects our thoughts and our character because we reflect on the past and the recording of all the negative actions and reactions start to replay like an old movie. We begin restoring broken places that have damaged us in so many ways with negative outcomes. We carry these same feelings into new relationships, which hinder us from giving ourselves wholeheartedly because we repeatedly play those old episodes of our lives as to *what* happened and *how* it happened.

There will always be a situation that resembles our past hurts. When we replay it, we think we must handle the new situation the same way we did the old, and by doing this we have allowed more and more walls to accumulate. This pattern becomes our safety net, and before we know it, we can't receive anything from anyone; we reject everything that comes our way. The castle we have built becomes our defense and our place of escape. To avoid this, there must be a conscious effort to allow healing to begin in our minds as well as our hearts.

Prayer

Father, God, I ask you to forgive me
for the things that I have held in my
heart that is not like you. Forgive
me of my trespasses, evil intentions,
hurtful things that have been said
out of my mouth and my bad
decisions. I pray for everyone that
our hearts may be healed, and
minds set free from past hurt. I pray
that every negative thought of the
past that has caused heartbreak,
anger, rage, discouragement,

sadness, disappointment,
murderous or other evil intention be
cast into the sea of forgetfulness.

I pray that chains are being broken
and that hands are no longer bound.
Help us to understand our purpose
as well as our identity in you. I
speak healing in the mind, body,
and soul from every situation and
circumstance that were hurtful and
caused sickness and disease.

I pray that families and friends be
restored from broken promises, false
hopes, bad influences,
manipulations, bad relationships
and anything else that may have
held us captive be washed away.
Every spirit of deceit, insensitivity,
misunderstanding, poverty, racism
and mind control, be cast down and
those affected be set free.

Help us to realize that we can
prosper in our mind, body, and soul.
Allow us to walk in the way that

You have purposed for our destiny. Father allow us to see ourselves as you see us, for we all have a destiny to fulfill. In Jesus name I pray. Amen and it is so.

Reference Notebook

What You Do Shows What You Are
The heart is meant to understand, discern, and give insight. The heart functions as the conscience.

"If you want good fruit, you must make the tree good. If your tree is not good, it will have bad fruit. A tree is known by the kind of fruit it produces. You snakes! You are so evil. How can you say anything good? What people say with their mouths comes from what fills their hearts."

Matthew 12:33-34

Our Hearts' Enemies are Guilt, Anger and Jealousy
Jeremiah 17:9

"He that trusteth in his own heart is a fool for who that is wise would trust one whom he knows to be desperately wicked?"

Guilt is what happens when you can't justify your own actions due to lapse in moral reasoning or regret of what could have been different.

Anger is a strong feeling of annoyance, displeasure, or hostility.

Jealousy is a feeling or display of envy toward someone because of what they possess or the perception thereof.

"You want things, but you don't get them. So you kill and are jealous of others."
James 4:2

Other Books by Mary Hale:

Emotional Baggage
The Walls of My Heart
The Castle of My Heart

Interested in having your
book published?
Contact APS Publishing

APS Books & More
2653 S. Lawndale
Chicago, IL 60623
847-942-6135
www.WeAreAPS.com

www.ingramcontent.com/pod-product-compliance
Lightning Source LLC
Chambersburg PA
CBHW031542040426
42445CB00010B/668